FIVE T'ANG POETS

FIELD TRANSLATION SERIES 15

Wang Wei
Li Po
Tu Fu
Li Ho
Li Shang-yin

FIVE T'ANG POETS

Translated and introduced
by David Young

Oberlin College Press:
FIELD Translation Series 15

Some of these translations, sometimes in different versions, appeared in the magazines *Choice, Field, Madrona, Malahat Review*, and *New Letters*; in two chapbooks, *Six Poems from Wang Wei* and *Magic Strings: 9 Poems from Li Ho*; and in the anthologies *The Confucian Vision* and *Light from the East*, both edited by William McNaughton, and *New Asian Writing*, edited by Judy and David Ray.

Publication of this book was made possible in part through a grant from the Ohio Arts Council.

Library of Congress Cataloging in Publication Data
    Wang Wei, Li Po, Tu Fu, Li Ho, Li Shang-yin
    (translated by David Young)
        Five T'ang Poets
        (The FIELD Translation Series; v. 15)
LC: 89–063738
ISBN: 0-932440-55-X

CONTENTS

LI PO

TU FU

PREFACE

This collection reflects a period of some fifteen years in which I have experimented with the intriguing problem of bringing Chinese poems over into English. My method has been to study the Chinese tradition as time and inclination have served; to translate when the impulse was strong and useful means and materials were available; and to check my results with friends and colleagues willing to bring their larger grasp of the subject and the language to bear on my efforts. My lines of approach have been as varied as I could make them: comparing existing translations, drawing upon scholarly discussions of texts I wanted to translate, working from literal (character-by-character) versions prepared by friends or available in published form; and learning as much as I could about Chinese grammar and poetic convention through collaborative translation (of a poet not included here) with a friend and former colleague.

It is useful to be clear on what this collection does and does not offer. It doesn't translate new materials; none of these poems appears here for

the first time in English. They have all been
translated previously, often several times; in-
deed, in selecting these four poets and represent-
ing them as I do, I am 'skimming the cream'
from the richest period of Chinese poetry, and I
would be the first to acknowledge that all four
poets, the middle two especially, have been
more extensively represented in English trans-
lation elsewhere. I am also happy to grant that
the translators who have dealt previously with
these poets have generally been better versed in
the language and background of the original
poems. My strength is on the side of English and
poetry. I feel that poets make good translators
because they can hope to construct effective
poems in the language into which the poem is
being rendered. No amount of scholarship and
erudition can substitute for that. A recent and
much-praised anthology of Chinese poetry in
translation, *Sunflower Splendor*, is laudable in its
accuracy and scholarship and generally deplor-
able in the quality of its English *as poetry* (though
it contains some notable exceptions to that judg-
ment). The poems do not really resemble any-
thing anyone would be apt to write as poetry
in English, with the result that they inadvertent-
ly make Chinese poetry look and sound rather

silly. It is the impulse to rescue my four poets from the often wooden and dogged versions of the scholars—or at least to supplement those versions with livelier and more limber counterparts—that lies behind this book. It can thus be said that I hope to take my place with other poets—Ezra Pound, Kenneth Rexroth and Gary Snyder, in particular, along with Arthur Waley, the scholar who translated like a poet—who have worked in Chinese translation. The ways in which that allegiance may be controversial will not in fact matter to most readers, who will be looking for readable and credible poems; it is the readers I hope to please, though not at the expense of a responsible attitude toward accurate representation of the poems I am trying to acquaint them with.

What are the particular problems of Chinese translation, and how have I attempted to solve them? We might begin by noting that a Chinese poem works like a kind of grid. Syntax moves along the line in one direction, while pleasing parallels and juxtapositions show up at right angles to that movement. When you try to duplicate this in English, you get an effect of stiff formality that disables the lyric voice of the poem. Here's an example from one of the Wang

Wei poems, first in a literal, character-by-character rendering:

stream	sound	swallow	dangerous	rocks
sun	color	cold	bluegreen	pines

Syntax is here represented as we would expect to see it, running horizontally, while the parallel juxtapositions can be seen operating vertically (it's the opposite in Chinese). In those parallel pairings nouns, verbs and adjectives are carefully matched, which helps us realize, for example, that "cold" is a verb, i.e. it has the same function as "swallow" in the line above. You could render these lines in English as follows:

> The sound of the stream is swallowed
> among huge rocks.
> The color of the sun is cold among
> bluegreen pines.

The syntactical duplication in English, along with the long end-stopped lines, produces a plodding and overformal effect that is one firm demonstration of the differences in music and movement between the two languages. The absence in Chinese of all that connective tissue of articles and prepositions makes the original grid airy and light, while its twin in English becomes musclebound and solemn.

Of course, most translators do not follow the formal parallelism that slavishly, but they are more influenced by it than they perhaps should be; here are three translations of those lines:

Fountains sob, swallowing perilous rocks.
Sun color chills green pines.

(Wai-lim Yip)

Sound of a stream choking on sharp rocks
Sun cool coloured among green pines—

(G. W. Robinson)

A gurgling stream chokes on treacherous
rocks;
The dying sun flicks coldly through the
blue pines.

(Chang Yin-nan & Lewis Walmsley)

The choices of diction vary, but the treatment of the lines is similar in all three cases: the English lines try to approximate the Chinese in length and structure, even though the effect is far less compelling. My own solution has been to admit that an English line is a different kind of unit and to treat the Chinese line like a stanza, breaking it up into smaller units of two or three lines. This allows me to preserve some of the parallelism while seeking a more supple and fluent movement. The grid effect, natural to one language and forced in the other, is gone, but the matched stanzas produce an effect that is somewhat equivalent in English without, I hope, sounding stilted:

then a little stream
gurgling
among gigantic rocks

even the color of sunlight
looks cool
coming through bluegreen pines

This rendering may also make more sense than the others. Of my three examples, the first seems to me to make sense only in a ludicrous way, while the others present problems of tone and exaggeration that seem inimical to the spirit of Wang Wei's poetry. None of them much resembles what somebody trying to write a poem in English would be apt to say, which must, I think, be one of the criteria for effective translation.

The reader will also have noticed the latitude of interpretation open to the translators in this example. Is it a stream or a fountain? Is it swallowing the rocks or are they swallowing it? Are the rocks perilous or sharp or treacherous; is that because they are large boulders? Are the pines blue or green or some combination of the two? And so it goes. There is no one right answer to such questions; they reflect a quality of the poetry that involves the reader in a more active role of interpretation than we are used to in our own poetic tradition, at least until very recently. That is a great part of the interest of Chinese poetry and a welcome opportunity to the translator, who has a little more operating room than he might have in working from another language. Have I, in deciding that the "dangerous" rocks were probably large boulders and in emphasizing their size, gone too far from the original? Perhaps I have. The existence of the other translations, playing it safer and losing the chance for an effective poem in English, along with my strong sense of the visual emphasis in Wang Wei's poetry, made me venturesome. My hope is that I am true to the spirit of Wang Wei while at the same time standing up for my rights as someone trying to create poetry in a different language and period.

Another problem for the translator of Chinese poetry is the multitude of place names and specialized references to be found in the poems. I have simply avoided trying to translate many poems because of the amount of material of that kind they contain. In the poems I have translated, I have left some such materials in, for the flavor they give the poems, and left others out, as not essential to the poem's meaning and success in English. In a few cases I have tried to incorporate into the poem itself explanatory phrases or interpretive elements that might otherwise show up in footnotes. The only extensive example is in Wang Wei's "Watching It Snow and Thinking of My Friend, the Hermit Hu," where the poet simply refers to the well-known (to him and his readers) story of Yüan An by naming the man, and I go on to tell enough of the story to make the reference comprehensible to English readers. That is the only case where I've added what amounts to the equivalent of a line in Chinese, but similar gestures of interpretation occur at other points, aiming to make footnotes unnecessary. This practice will seem odd to some, but the idea of poems that can stand on their own, without need of additional explanation, is one that other poets and most readers will, I think, find attractive.

Because I have written individual introductions for each poet, I shall not discuss them here except to note that, despite their many differences, they share a rich and exciting period in the history of their country and culture. Their appeal to us lies not only in their greatness as individual poets, but in the peculiar strengths of their tradition—faith in the power of juxtaposed images, trust in the effectiveness of implication, an immediacy and directness in the use of voice—that we have adopted as cardinal values of modern poetry. To me it is a matter of continual wonder and delight that poetry written some twelve centuries ago, on the other side of the world in a vastly different civilization, should speak to us with such freshness and force. That poems can survive so long and claim their imaginative kinship with us affords a useful perspective on our own time and place, and moves us profoundly by confronting us with the human ability to share and communicate emotion and experience through language. Such fundamental facts about an enterprise of this kind are always worth reiterating.

I have many people to thank, and am anxious that they should share credit for whatever may be positive here without risking blame for any of my errors or shortcomings. William Mc-Naughton is the former colleague whose collaborative work taught me so much about Chinese language and literature. Others who have lent their expertise in Chinese at various points along the way are Richard Kent, Ch'ui Shu-hua Kent, Mary Anne Cartelli, Dale Johnson, and Hugh M. Stimson. Readers who have helped me with the English side of things include all of the above as well as my wife Chloe, Stuart Friebert, David Walker, and Bruce Weigl. I especially want to thank Stuart Friebert for stirring me up to finish this book, and Barbara Marshall for her help in typing the manuscript.

Oberlin
June, 1980

For this second edition, expanded by the addition of fourteen poems by Li Shang-yin, I wish to add new thanks to Stuart Friebert, for encouraging the project, and to Dale Johnson, for his literal versions of Li Shang-yin and his suggestions for improvement in my translations.

Oberlin
November, 1989

WANG WEI

WANG WEI

The landscape is everything. It contains everything, including the poet, who is often simply an entranced, silent watcher. Nature brims with magic and mystery, but its overtones are neither anthropomorphic nor supernatural. A poised, confident naturalism has replaced human animism, and that is a cause for rejoicing. Or mostly so; just occasionally is there a hint of being not so much excluded as simply very small, lost in the size and majesty of the landscape with a tangle of slightly irrelevant feelings. More often, the sense of wonder and the trance of acceptance predominate, and the emotional 'startle,' the sudden tug of recollection and sadness that ends some of the poems, does not counteract the poised serenity but is rather absorbed into it. A Western poet might want the landscape to reflect his or her feelings and react with sorrow or even despair if it did not; a Chinese poet of landscape, and Wang Wei seems the example *par excellence*, is willing simply to know that his feelings, however disparate, are allowed to be part of the whole.

The claim that Wang Wei was the father of Chinese landscape painting is somewhat mysterious—only copies survive, and earlier masters can be identified—and some art historians have thought it exaggerated; but like so many legends that attach to the great originals of the Chinese cultural tradition, it is apposite when we consider how completely this painter-poet seems to have been able to entrust his art to the depiction of landscape for its own sake and in its own terms. Sherman Lee says of one of Wang Wei's paintings that "the organization is additive and consists of a series of space cells enclosing the principal points of interest." That is a useful description of the poems, and I have tried to reflect such qualities by my use of space and movement. We stand on a lookout point or climb a mountain or float on water with the poet, and our attention, like his, is directed steadily to one thing, or set of things, at a time—above and below, near and distant, huge next to small. Natural process—the passing of daylight, the permutations of weather, the great wheel of the seasons —occurs slowly and majestically. And the poems are written with a confidence that steady observation and cumulative absorption of the surroundings will be fully rewarded and rewarding.

We are told that *forms* are the true subject of Chinese landscape painting, and it is exciting to notice how Wang Wei concentrates on them in his poems: the large and sumptuous shapes of clouds and mountains, the small and delicate forms of moving water, pine needles, willow fluff. Yet it is useful too to see that the poet does one thing the painter cannot; he uses sound. In most of these poems there is an extremely canny placement of sound, often in the distance, and its presence helps us sense and appreciate the silence that surrounds it. In the use of sound to counterpoise the emphasis on the visual we have perhaps an equivalent to the small and sometimes melancholy human figures that are nearly lost in the vast natural panoramas; it gives a relish to the whole that we understand and accept intuitively, instantaneously, and with a rush of pleasure that the poet has of course planned for us, working with care and with an emotion that might best be called piety. We are reminded that Wang Wei was a reverent Buddhist. But no careful reader needs to be told that these are the poems of a deeply religious sensibility, and no label needs to be attached to their sense of devotion. Its 'calligraphy' is what we care about—the shape, the poise, the texture and simple order of each poem.

Wang Wei's life, variously dated as 699-759 or 761, and 701-761, included an early success at court and in the capital, a fall from favor and a short career as a minor official, a semi-retirement to his estate on the Wang river (destined to be made famous by his poetry), and the early death of his wife. It was a life in which periods of retirement and solitude were interspersed with official duties and travels. In his later years Wang Wei was embroiled in a rebellion and forced to take sides, with some danger to his life, but he survived this period of social chaos and died peacefully, honored by his many friends and by the state.

Something like four hundred poems by Wang Wei survive. All the ones I have chosen were written in one of his characteristic forms, of eight lines, with five characters to the line. He was also master of shorter forms, however, and he liked linked sequences and groups of poems in which two poets took turns responding to a subject and to each other. Readers who want to explore his work in English translation will find three recent collections of his work: *Poems by Wang Wei*, translated by Chang Yin-nan and Lewis C. Walmsley (Tuttle, 1958); *Hiding the Universe*, translated by Wai-lim Yip (Grossman-Mushinsha, 1972); and *Poems by Wang Wei*, translated by G. W. Robinson (Penguin, 1973).

A SPRING DAY AT THE FARM

Pigeons coo on the roof
apricot orchards
bloom white at the edge of town

the farmers are out with axes
pruning the mulberry trees
hoeing watercourses

swallows hunt up old nests
old men sit in the sun
almanacs on their laps

I have forgotten my glass of wine
thinking of lost friends,
                              dead friends,
in a blaze of old pain.

WATCHING THE HUNT

The wind blows
the horn-bow twangs

the general is hunting
beyond Wei city

withered grasses
give the falcons
sharper eyes

snowless ground
lets the horses
gallop free

the hunters canter past our village
headed for camp

they rein in, looking back
to where they shot down eagles

flat clouds
a thousand miles of evening.

TO SECRETARY SU

My place is at the mouth of the valley
beyond tall trees
around an empty village

you came down that stony road
for nothing

no one to meet you
at my cottage

fishing boats were stuck
on the frozen riverbank

a hunting fire was burning on the plain

the night was white
and silent

only the howls of gibbons
and a far-off temple bell.

AUTUMN EVENING IN THE MOUNTAINS

After the rain
that covered these mountains
the night air
smells of fall

the moon gleams
among long-needled pines

rushing softly across its rocks
the creek
glitters

bringing their laundry home
through the bamboos
women chatter

a fisherman poles his boat
through the heavy lotus leaves
swaying

the spring flowers
and their heavy <u>odors</u>
are gone

stick around anyway
<u>old friend</u>
for the beauty of fall.

WALKING IN MOUNTAINS IN THE RAIN

In this quick cloudburst
air thickens, the sky comes down — *rain*

dark mountains
flashes of lightning — *thunder storm*

out at sea new clouds
have just started to form
and this small brook I straddle
is a river in flood somewhere — *flooding*

rags and blankets of mist — *fog*
hang on these slopes and cliffs

then the clouds open and vanish
rain patters off   *storm ends*
and moonlight silvers
that whole reach of river
foothills to ocean

and even from this black mountain   *world*
I can hear boatmen singing.   *becomes*
                                      happy

32

LATE SPRING: MR. YEN AND HIS FRIENDS
COME TO VISIT

Pines grow here
also chrysanthemums
along my wild paths

books in the house
by the cartload

I roast some sunflower seeds
to treat these distinguished guests
who have stopped by
on their bamboo viewing tour

birds were nesting here
before the spring turned green
and the orioles sing on
after the petals have fallen

but I have to admit I'm a little sad
about the whiteness of my hair
as if I couldn't quite accept
all the pleasures of this season.

MY MOUNT CHUNGNAN COTTAGE

Since middle age I've been
a most enthusiastic Buddhist

now that I'm old I've settled
here in the mountain country

sometimes I get so happy
I have to go off by myself

there are marvelous places
I alone know about

I climb
to the source of a stream

and sit
to watch the rising mists

sometimes I come across
an old man of the woods

we talk and laugh
and forget to go home.

SPRING IN THE GARDEN

After a night of rain
I go out, wearing clogs

wrapped in an old overcoat
against the spring cold

water pours white
through the open dikes

peach blossoms glow red
beyond the willows

fields of new grass spread away
edged and checkered

poles rise from the wells
at the wood's edge

I go back in
to write at my small desk

evening arrives, I'm alone
happy among green weeds.

WATCHING IT SNOW AND THINKING
OF MY FRIEND, THE HERMIT HU

The drum thumps
for a cold
thin dawn

squinting
I peer at my lined face
in the bright mirror

beyond the shutter
wind
rattling the bamboo

I open the door—
snow covers the hills
for miles

the sky has come down
lying peacefully
in the deep lanes and byways

white drifts rise
in the silent
courtyards

I think of Yüan An, long ago
who starved and froze
rather than bother rescuers

is that how you are now
silent
behind closed doors?

PASSING THE TEMPLE OF
ACCUMULATED FRAGRANCE

I didn't know the way to the temple
so I walked miles
among the cloudy peaks

walked through primeval forests
no path
not even a footprint

deep in the mountains
I heard a bell—
where did it come from?

then a little stream
gurgling
among gigantic rocks

even the color of sunlight
looks cool
coming through bluegreen pines

at dusk I knelt
next to a small
deserted lake

meditating
to chase away
the poison dragon of emotion.

RETURNING TO MY COTTAGE

A bell in the distance
the sound floats
down the valley

one by one
woodcutters and fisherman
stop work, start home

the mountains move off
into darkness

alone, I turn home
as great clouds beckon
from the horizon

the wind stirs delicate vines
and water chestnut shoots
catkin fluff sails past

in the marsh to the east
new growth
vibrates with color

it's sad
to walk in the house
and shut the door.

FLOATING ON A MARSH

Autumn
the sky huge and clear
the marsh miles from farms and houses

overjoyed by the cranes
standing around the sandbar

the mountains above the clouds in the distance

this water
utterly still
in the dusk

the white moon overhead

I let my boat drift free tonight
I can't go home.

LI PO

LI PO

He seems half-man, half-myth. The personality that informs the poems and that is haloed by a long tradition of deep affection may once have been less than legendary, but it can never have been ordinary. The Chinese have valued Li Po for his gaiety, freedom, sympathy and energy for so long that he has become a sort of archetype of the bohemian artist and puckish wanderer. The story that he drowned when he drunkenly tried to embrace the moon in the river is doubtless apocryphal, but it is also delightfully apt to anyone who knows his work; and the scholar who protested that the poem addressed to Tu Fu could not be by Li Po because the latter would never address the former with such levity and disrespect was laboring under a misplaced notion of decorum. The stories that have come down to us, whether legend or fact, have an effective way of integrating the life of the man and the spirit of the work, perhaps the nicest kind of gift that posterity can bestow on a poet.

A number of these poems are about drinking and being drunk, and while that theme is not exclusive to Li Po, it is one he is obviously particularly comfortable with. That partly tells us how much Li Po enjoyed his wine, but since lots of poets like to drink without ever feeling moved to write about it, we also need to see how it serves him as a poetic metaphor. Life at its best, as Li Po envisions it, is a kind of intoxication, an elevation; poetry, like good wine, should help us get perspective on ourselves and put the cares of the world aside. Even nature, as Li Po likes to present it, has a kind of intoxicated quality, especially in spring. The poet's presentation of himself as drunkenly enjoying some natural setting is thus a cleverly unpretentious way of presenting transcendent states of mind and being. This idea isn't exclusive to Li Po, but he handles the metaphor of the bibulous poet in a tipsy world as well as anyone before or since.

We can get some notion of Li Po's distinctive voice and manner if we compare his "climbing" poem, "High in the Mountains, I Fail to Find the Wise Man," with a comparable Wang Wei poem, "Passing the Temple of Accumulated Fragrance." Both poets present themselves as wandering around half-lost in the mountains, looking for someone or something sacred. Wang Wei's progression of images is sure and exciting, moving to the quiet closure with the speaker meditating next to a still pond or lake as the evening comes on. Whether he has also found the temple scarcely seems to matter, since he has found, in effect, the peace of mind he was presumably searching for. Li Po's poem begins more abruptly, moves forward more unpredictably, and ends more astonishingly. Its movements from image to image seem like slightly larger leaps, and each image or sensation—the sight of the deer, the sudden sky overhead, the breathtakingly beautiful sight of the waterfall—is charged with delight and magic. The ending (if my interpretation of it is correct) is a more striking version of Wang Wei's idea: after this set of experiences, any upset or "grief" about failing in his original purpose is almost comically irrelevant. Each poet has his own strengths: Wang Wei's sure sense of detail and ability to pull a poem together around its closing image are especially impressive, along with his subtle handling of tone. In Li Po's case, there is a greater willingness to be centrifugal, to let the poem scatter in several directions, a risky tendency that fits nicely with the metaphoric "intoxication" I have spoken of, and that is surely one source of the legend of Li Po as carefree wanderer and social misfit.

Another difference from Wang Wei can be found in Li Po's willingness to cast poems in the voices of people other than himself. The most famous example is the great poem Ezra Pound translated under the title "The River Merchant's Wife: A Letter." My own examples are the little poem titled "She Thinks of Him" and the poem spoken by soldiers, " 'We Fought South of the Ramparts.' " The first example serves to demonstrate how convincingly Li Po could speak through the sensibility and experience of a woman; the second shows the social and political insights he was capable of. Both are part of a larger tendency to sympathize with the world and people he encountered, an ability to enter fully into the experiences of others. This ability also gave Li Po his keen appreciation of the value of friendship. Like Wang Wei, he has times of solitude in which he appreciates total isolation, and, again like Wang Wei, he likes to balance such moments with company and conviviality. But the appreciation of the company of others that is somewhat ceremonious and guarded in Wang Wei becomes a heartfelt enthusiasm for friends and a genuine distress at parting from them in Li Po. Moments of separation fascinate him because of the challenge they present to his pursuit of elation, and his solutions, or resolutions, are poignant and various. Again, we are talking about one poet's handling of what was already a tradition—poems of friendship and leavetaking were a standard type by Li Po's time—but the distinctiveness and authenticity of that handling are among the hallmarks of Li Po's work.

Most of the experts now date Li Po's birth as 701, which would make him the same age as Wang Wei, and some eleven years older than Tu Fu. He seems to have been born outside of China, perhaps in present-day Afghanistan, but in any case he grew up in the mountainous south-western province of Szechwan. As a boy he showed what would become a lifelong interest in meditation and spiritual discipline by going off to study with a hermit known as the Master of the Eastern Cliff. He was also, as a young man, something of a swordsman. His gifts eventually took him to the capital and the service of the Emperor, but he was too unruly for court life, and soon resumed his routine of travel, study, drinking bouts, and writing. During the period of civil war he fell in with a rebellious prince of the royal family and was imprisoned for a time. He died in relative poverty, famous in his own lifetime as an unusually gifted poet in a nation of poets.

The man who emerges from the poems and from the scraps of contemporary accounts was certainly not without flaws of character. He was boastful, given to exaggeration and downright lying, and irresponsible as a father, husband, and citizen. His status as a social misfit equipped him for the life of a recluse or monk, but unfortunately he had expensive tastes and loved good company, expensive wine, and dancing girls. He never stood for the Civil Service exams, an extraordinary thing when we recall that success in them depended so much upon poetic ability. As Arthur Waley puts it:

> The poems, then, are those of a man who in the eyes of a society largely dominated by bureaucratic values had completely failed in his career or rather had failed to have a career at all. There were poets who had lost their jobs and poets who after a time had returned voluntarily to private life. But that a great poet should never have had a job at all was almost unprecedented. Some people no doubt thought that such a situation was highly discreditable to the Government. Others,

like Wei Hao, believed that to have given him a job would only have been asking for trouble. Li Po himself, in a poem addressed to his wife, confesses that his drunkenness made him as good as no husband at all; but he never seems to have faced the fact that it also disqualified him for official service.

What is striking about all this is that admiration for the poet had already begun to overshadow reservations about the man in Li Po's own lifetime, as it has certainly continued to do since.

To a highly tradition-bound poetry, Li Po brought a sense of freedom and adventure. He showed an extraordinary ability to exploit the openness of the Chinese language, its gaps and implications, so that, reading his direct and simple poems, we find ourselves supplying their richness and exploring their implications. Arthur Cooper speaks of the way the line that translates literally as "*drunk rise stalk brook moon*" in the poem I have called "Indulgence" ("Abandon" is Cooper's title) fills out in our imaginations so that we know what kind of landscape it is set in and find ourselves acting it out and participating in its emotions to a surprising degree. One could multiply such examples endlessly. Li Po has an intuitive grasp of the genius of his language and its possibilities for poetry, and it is his exploitation of this understanding that allows us to return again and again to his apparently simple and unpretentious poems for refreshment, imaginative exhilaration, and a sense of their capacity to outlast the limitations of the life and circumstances that produced them.

Readers who wish to explore Li Po's work further will of course find him in all of the standard anthologies of Chinese poetry such as Robert Payne's *The White Pony* (New American Library, 1947) and *Sunflower Splendor* (Anchor, 1975). Arthur Waley's biography, *The Poetry and Career of Li Po* (Allen and Unwin, 1950), cited above, is a bit dour but highly informative, and it provides, as one would expect, some impressive translations along the way. An earlier book, *The Works of Li Po, The Chinese Poet* (E. P. Dutton, 1922), translated by Shigeyoshi Obata, has merits of its own. The Li Po of the longer poems, dream poems and extended narratives, can of course be discovered in the brilliant translations of Pound (see especially his version of "Exile's Letter"), but is also effectively represented in Arthur Cooper's *Li Po and Tu Fu* (Penguin, 1973).

A CLEAR WET DAWN

Cool fields
the thin rain
stops

spring in every direction

blue pond
swarms with fish

thrushes sing
in the green branches

flowers look tear-streaked

grass in high meadows
bends level

through the bamboo
in the still stream
you can see
the last shreds of cloud
scattering
in the dawn wind

DRINKING IN MOONLIGHT

I sit with my wine jar
among flowers
blossoming trees

no one to drink with

well, there's the moon

I raise my cup
and ask him to join me
bringing my shadow
making us three

but the moon doesn't seem to be drinking
and my shadow just creeps around behind me

still, we're companions tonight
me, the moon, and the shadow
we're observing
the rites of spring

I sing
and the moon rocks back and forth

I dance
and my shadow
weaves and tumbles with me

we celebrate for awhile
then go our own ways, drunk

may we meet again someday
in the white river of stars
overhead!

FOR TU FU

On Boiled Rice Mountain
I met Tu Fu

wearing a big round
bamboo hat
in the hot noon sun

Tu Fu
how come
you've grown
so thin?

you must be suffering
too much
from poetry!

GROTTO GARDEN

From the grotto in the garden I can see
the fall moon
shining west above the lake

from north of the river
the wild geese
are leaving early

singing a song about white flowers
drunken travelers
crowd their boat

they scarcely notice
the dew and mist
that soak their autumn clothing

TAKING LEAVE OF A FRIEND

Here at the city wall
green mountains to the north
white water winding east
we part

one tumbleweed
ten thousand miles to go

high clouds
wandering thoughts

sunset
old friendship

you wave, moving off
your horse
whinnies
twice

LISTENING TO THE MONK CHUN
PLAY HIS LUTE

A monk from Szechwan
comes out of the mountains
with a famous antique lute

he strums the strings once
and I hear the wind
through a thousand valley pines

a traveler's heart
is rinsed
in flowing water

the echo mingles
with temple bells
in frosty air

evening
comes without warning
into these green hills

autumn clouds
darkening
who knows how many layers.

SHE THINKS OF HIM

I'm a peach tree
deep in a gorge, flowering
smiling and nodding to no one

you were the moon
high in the night sky
shining down on me one hour
and then going on

a razorsharp sword
can't cut a stream of water
it foams across the blade, goes on

my thoughts don't stop
they are the stream
they flow
they follow you forever

'FIGHTING SOUTH OF THE RAMPARTS'

1

Last year we fought
at the headwaters
of the Mulberry

this year we're fighting
on the Onion River Road

we have washed our swords
in the Caspian Sea

pastured our horses
in Himalayan snows

we're the Emperor's armies
growing old, getting gray
ten thousand miles from home.

2

It's all right for the Huns
battle's like farming to them

and the crops in their yellow deserts
are skulls and bleached bones.

3

The House of Ch'in
built the Great Wall
to keep the Tartars out

the House of Han
keeps the signal fires lit

the beacons never go out
and the war never seems to stop

hand to hand, swords flashing
men grapple and die in the field
horses fall, their squeals
drift skyward

the crows and kites
peck for human guts
carry them off in their beaks
and hang them on dead trees

soldiers and captains smeared
on desert shrubs and grass.

4

What have the generals accomplished?
what they know
is less than what we've learned—

a sword's a stinking thing
a wise man will use
as seldom as he can.

GOODBYE AT THE RIVER

In this little river town
the autumn rain lets up
the wine's all gone
well then, goodbye!

you stretch out in your boat
the sail fills, you skim home
past islands burning with flowers
banks crowded with willows

what about me? I don't know
I think I'll go sit
on that big rock
and fish

64

TO WANG LUN

I was just
shoving off
in my boat

when I heard
someone stomping
and singing on the shore!

Peach Blossom Lake
is a thousand feet deep

but it can't compare
with Wang Lun's love
or the way he said
goodbye

HIGH IN THE MOUNTAINS,
I FAIL TO FIND THE WISE MAN

In the distance I can hear
a dog barking
and the sound of fast water

rain-filled peach blossoms
shower me as I walk

sometimes, deep in the trees,
I glimpse a stag

standing by a creek at noon
I can't hear
a single bell

overhead the wild bamboos
divide a cloud-blue sky

a flying spring
hangs a white plume
from a jade-green peak

he's gone, they don't know where
I lean my grief
on two or three pines
and walk away

LITTLE ELEGY

That madman from the eastern regions
Ho Chi-chang
wild as wind and river

first time I met him
at the capital
he called me 'angel in exile'

oh how he loved his cup
and now he's dirt
under the pine trees

he pawned his gold turtle
to buy me wine

as I remember that
tears wet my scarf.

CONVERSATION AMONG MOUNTAINS

You ask why I live
in these green mountains

I smile
can't answer

I am completely at peace

a peach blossom
sails past
on the current

there are worlds
beyond this one

WAKING UP DRUNK ON A SPRING DAY

Life is a huge dream
why work so hard?

all day long I drink
lying outside the front door

awakening
looking up through the trees
in the garden

and one bird singing in the flowers

70

bird, what season is this?
"Spring! I'm a mango bird
and the spring wind makes me sing."

now I grow sad
very sad

so I have some more wine
and I sing
out loud
until the bright moon
rises

what was I upset about?
I can't remember

INDULGENCE

Absorbed with my wine
I didn't notice
the twilight

my clothes
were covered
with fallen petals

drunk I rose up
and trailed the moon
in the quiet creek

birds gone
people few

72

BLUE WATER SONG

Blue water
burning moon

on South Lake
he gathers lillies

the lotus flowers
whisper

the lone boatman
sighs

AUTUMN LINES

Clean fall wind
clear fall moon

leaves heaped by the wind
leaves scattered

a cold raven
flaps slowly
from his roost

thoughts of you
fill my head

will I ever
see you again?

the ache
around my heart
gets bigger

74

TU FU

TU FU

The widely held view that Tu Fu is China's greatest poet is partly based on admiration for his technical brilliance, a fluent mastery of traditional forms combined with an originality that gives rise to apparently effortless innovation; Yeats in our own time provides an analogy, and Keats is a similar instance among the Romantics. These qualities will not be apparent in translations, and neither in my versions nor in others I have seen does Tu Fu's formal excellence distinguish him significantly from other Chinese poets. But a poet's greatness, especially the kind of ultimate tribute accorded to Tu Fu, is never founded solely on craft and technique; ultimately, the poet's vision of existence is what wins readers, and if the refinements of expression and form associated with his own language and tradition are apt to be lost in the change from one language to another, the fundamental means of his poetry—the images and their relationships and the world they serve to create—can, fortunately, be reflected, so that a large portion of his essential genius is recreated and preserved. Tu Fu is a great-minded, great-hearted poet with a commanding imagination, qualities a translator can still hope to capture.

Adversity was certainly one source of the greatness. Until his middle years Tu Fu was a poet of undeniable talent, but, on the evidence of his work, a somewhat boastful and querulous man, concerned mainly about his career and lack of advancement, and rather given to feeling sorry for himself. He received some patronage and official recognition, but never enough to satisfy him. His bitterness began to take the form of social criticism and a new concern for the sufferings of others. (His own woes were not after all very significant in comparison.) This growing tendency toward compassion and widening sense of the tragic features of the human condition were then given a tremendous impetus by the historical events in which he was suddenly caught up. His little son starved to death in a famine before Tu Fu was able to get to his family and help them. The An Lu-shan rebellion broke out, and the poet fled with his wife and two children to a safer place. Tu Fu fell into the hands of the rebels and was held for some time in the captured capital. Eventually he escaped and rejoined the exile court, but it was some time before he was reunited with his family. These experiences, in the midst of social chaos that affected everyone he saw, gave him enormous compassion for the sufferings of poor people, soldiers, and scattered families. He became a great poet, transcending self-pity and setting even his poems about pleasure in an implicit frame of pain.

That we know enough to say all this about Tu Fu is due to the fact that he was a man of extraordinary candor. His poetry is more autobiographical, and more honest about his failings and feelings, than any poet's had managed to be before. He documented his own life in great detail, placing it in the contexts of both historical change and day-to-day life, in the capital and in provincial villages throughout the empire, so that we have in his total output (the largest corpus of any of the four poets in this collection, something around 1,400 poems) a remarkably complete portrait not only of the man but of his time and place as well. It is, we feel, an unvarnished and vividly observed account; listening to Tu Fu narrate some circumstance of his life, such as his flight with his family from the rebel troops, we feel that experience is being transcribed effortlessly and candidly; it is as though we were in the presence of the man himself, as he tells his story, or, often, as though the experiences were our own and we were living through them. Part of that great technical accomplishment was a naturalness of manner and style that wins readers and creates a special bond with them. It is art so magical that we have to stop to remind ourselves that it *is* art, compounded of contrivance and calculation. Yeats's ideal comes to mind: "A line will take us hours maybe; / Yet if it does not seem a moment's thought, / Our stitching and unstitching has been naught." That would have appealed to Tu Fu, who strove always for an overall effect of spontaneity.

The end of the rebellion saw Tu Fu back in the capital for a brief period of royal favor and government office, but he was soon exiled to an outlying province, and the post he held there did not suit him; within a few years he had abandoned it and begun another period of moving his family around in search of food, shelter, and peace of mind. For a few years he lived rather happily in a thatched hut, writing poetry of a bucolic sort, but further rebellions and disruptions kept him on the move and living hand ιο mouth for most of the rest of his life. From his own point of view, Tu Fu was a failed and disappointed man; from ours, he was enjoying years of incredible poetic productivity and development. We who see literature as an end in itself find it difficult to understand why Tu Fu would think of himself as a failed writer because his life had included no significant public service. But the Confucian ideals that associated the two things were so strong in his mind that he could never rid himself of them.

His response to this situation, if it was partly disappointment, was a sense of artistic independence; he could write to please himself and express his feelings, and it probably made a greater and more individual poet of him. "Poetry," as A. R. Davis puts it, "became the central preoccupation of his life, and he became more nearly a professional poet." Had Tu Fu realized his ambition to be a high government official in the capital, he would not have traveled as he did, and thus would not have written the marvelous body of travel poetry that portrays the China of his time so effectively; he would have associated far less with ordinary people, peasants, artisans, and soldiers, and thus been far less able to reflect their lives and speak to their sufferings; and, as he would have been a more conventional man, he would probably have remained a more conventional writer. It's both hindsight and speculation to say that we owe this great poet to the woes that beset him and his country in the middle of the eighth century, but something of that kind does seem to be the case.

Almost all commentators remark on the range of Tu Fu's poetry. His subjects are those of other poets, but unlike other poets, he seems to cover them all. The same can be said of the range of his themes and his tones. He is a comprehensive poet whose imagination seems capable of taking on almost anything. We value him, quite rightly, for his realism, directness, and candor. But we should also recognize his artfulness, the cunning management of the medium and of the reader's response that must characterize the work of any great writer. Most of all, I suppose, we associate Tu Fu with a vigorous poetry that manages to transcend unhappiness and melancholy by its enormous range and immense humanity.

Tu Fu has been blessed with a wealth of translators and commentators. I have already mentioned Arthur Cooper's *Li Po and Tu Fu* (Penguin, 1973). Some of Tu Fu's later work is to be

found in A. C. Graham's *Poems of the Late T'ang*.
He is also represented in Kenneth Rexroth's
memorable *One Hundred Poems from the Chinese*
(New Directions, 1956). Among the books en-
tirely devoted to Tu Fu, my own favorites are
David Hawkes's *A Little Primer of Tu Fu* (Oxford,
1967), which gives poems in transliteration,
character-by-character translation, and prose
paraphrase with accompanying notes and com-
ments—a translator's delight; A. R. Davis's
biography, *Tu Fu* (Twayne, 1971); William
Hung's two volume *Tu Fu, China's Greatest Poet*
(Harvard, 1952), a biography with very exten-
sive prose translations of the poetry; and Erwin
von Zach's *Tu Fu's Gedichte* (Harvard, 1952),
which contains *all* the poems in German transla-
tions. Other studies include Underwood and
Chu, *Tu Fu, Wanderer and Minstrel under Moons of
Cathay* (Mosher, 1929); Florence Ayscough's *Tu
Fu, the Autobiography of a Chinese Poet* (Jonathan
Cape and Houghton Mifflin, 1929, 1934, 2 vols.);
and Alley and Chih, *Tu Fu, Selected Poems* (Pek-
ing Foreign Language Press, 1964).

from FIVE HUNDRED WORDS ABOUT
MY JOURNEY FROM THE CAPITAL
TO FENG-HSIEN

(written just before the great rebellion of 755
broke out)

Year's end, the grasses withered
a great wind scouring the high ridges
in bitter cold at midnight I set out
along the Imperial highway

sharp frost, my belt snaps
my fingers are too stiff to tie it

around dawn I pass
the emperor's favorite winter palace
in the Li Hills by the hot springs

lots of army banners against the sky
the ground tramped smooth by troops

thick steam rises
from the hot green springs
Imperial guards rub elbows
cabinet ministers live it up

the music drifts through the wintry landscape

the hot baths here
are just for important people
nothing for common folks

the silk the courtiers wear
was woven by poor women
soldiers beat their husbands
demanding tribute

of course our emperor is generous
he only wants the best for us
I suppose we have to blame his ministers
when government is bad

plenty of good people at the court
must be worried
especially when they see the palace gold plate
carted off by royal relations

women like goddesses
are dancing inside
all silk and perfume
guests in sable furs
music of pipes and fiddles
camel-pad broth being served
with frosted oranges and pungent tangerines

behind those red gates
meat and wine are left to spoil
outside lie the bones
of people who starved and froze
luxury and misery a few feet apart!

my heart aches to think about it.

A MOONLIT NIGHT

Tonight
in this same moonlight
my wife is alone at her window

I can hardly bear to think of my children
too young to understand
why I can't come to them

her hair must be damp from the mist
her arms cold jade in the moonlight

when will we stand together
by those slack curtains
while the moonlight
dries the tear-streaks
on our faces?

SPRING SCENE

The state goes to ruin
mountains and rivers survive

spring in the city
thick leaves   deep grass

in times like these
the flowers seem to weep

birds, as if they too
hated separation
flutter close by
startle the heart

for three months
the beacon fires
have been burning

a letter from home
is worth a fortune

this white hair
is getting so sparse
from scratching
pretty soon
it will be too thin
to hold a hatpin!

THE P'ENG-YA ROAD

I remember when we fled from the rebels
heading north through danger and hardship
starting out in the middle of the night
with the moon shining on the Po-shui hills
and all of us on foot

whenever we met people on the road
we felt ashamed

now and then birds sang in the ravines

no one was going in the opposite direction

my silly little daughter
bit me in her hunger—
afraid that her crying would bring tigers
I held her mouth against my chest
she wriggled free and cried louder

my son acted like he knew
what it was all about
but he kept trying to eat
the bitter plums on the roadside trees

ten days we went, half that time
through thunderstorms
struggling to help each other in the mud
we had no protection from the rain
the road was too slippery
our clothes were too thin
some days we couldn't cover
more than a couple of miles
our food was wild berries
our shelter was low branches
mornings we waded the flooded creeks
evenings we crouched in mist at the sky's edge

we stopped near T'ung-chia Marsh
before crossing the high pass
and my friend Sun Tsai
took us in

his generosity reaches to the clouds

we arrived in pitch dark
they lit the lamps, opened the gates
brought warm water to bathe our feet
cut silhouettes and burned them
calling back our frightened spirits

his wife and children came out to greet us
when they saw how we looked they burst into tears
my children, exhausted, had fallen asleep
we woke them so they could eat
from the platters of food
"You and I," Sun Tsai said,
"will be sworn brothers"
and the hall was put at our disposal
and we were told to feel at home

in these bad times
where do you find
that kind of trust?

it's a year since we left there
the Tartars are still on the rampage
Sun Tsai, I wish I had wings
so I could fly
straight to your house
and see you again!

MEANDERING RIVER

1

Every fallen petal
diminishes spring

so the wind showers down a thousand
just to make me sad

I'll keep my eyes
on the ones that remain

and have some wine
whether it's good for me or not

kingfishers nest
in the ruins by the river

a stone unicorn
lies on its side in the park

Nature says, Enjoy yourself
and don't waste time

why worry then
about things like rank and office?

2

Daily, after Court
I take my clothes to the pawnshop

every night
I come back from the riverbank, drunk

I have an unpaid bill
in every tavern

well, who lives to be seventy
anyway?

butterflies
deep in the flowers

dragonflies
flicking the river's surface

let them all go on
time and the wind and the light

since we're told not to defy them
let's enjoy them while we can!

FOR LI PO

The cloud floats off
the way the sun went
the traveler doesn't come back

three nights in a row
I dreamed of you, old friend
so real I could have touched you!

you left in a hurry
I'll bet
you're having a bad journey

storms come up fast
on those rivers and lakes
don't fall out of your boat!

leaving, framed in the doorway
you scratched your snowy head
I knew you didn't want to go

bureaucrats
fatten in the capital
while a poet goes cold and hungry

if there is justice in heaven
what sent you out
to banishment?

ages to come
will warm themselves
at your verses

but it's
a cold, silent world
you left behind

IN THE CITY ON BUSINESS I MEET ONE FRIEND AND WE SPEND THE NIGHT EATING AND DRINKING AT THE HOUSE OF ANOTHER

1

A high wind
blows dust through the river districts
travelers pass
hands over eyes
unrecognized

east of the city
I open my eyes
and there, as I tie up my horse
I see Yun Ching!

Let's go see
Liu Hao—
it'll be worth
the extra trip.

2

Taking our hands
he leads us in
lights lamps
pours wine
sets out dish after dish

"Let's talk all night," he says
"and live it up,
and not one word about the war!"

3

The stove burns red
like a tiny dawn
and the moon outside
makes the paper window
shine like rippled silk

a while ago
the uproar at the capital
turned the whole world on its head
now winter's over, spring has begun
even around the palace walls

who'd have thought our tracks
would cross again like this?
where's the time got to?
and why is life

so full of goodbyes?

as we part in the yard
roosters are crowing in the trees
and we cry a little
drunk and happy
tears threading our cheeks.

THINKING OF MY BROTHERS ON A MOONLIT NIGHT

Garrison drums
stop travel

autumn on the frontier
sound of one wild goose

nightfall   from now on
the dew will be white

this same moon shines
where I grew up

my brothers are scattered
no way to know if they're alive

the letters we send each other
never seem to arrive

and the war goes on and on.

NEW MOON

Such a thin moon!
in its first quarter

a slanting shadow
a partly finished ring

barely risen
over the ancient fort

hanging at the edge
of the evening clouds

the Milky Way
hasn't changed color

the mountain passes
are cold and empty

there's white dew
in the front courtyard

secretly filling
the drenched carnations.

RAIN ON A SPRING NIGHT

Congratulations, rain
you know when to fall

coming at night, quiet
walking in the wind

making sure things
get good and wet

the clouds hang dark
over country roads

there's one light from a boat
coming downriver

in the morning
everything's dripping

red flowers
everywhere

SEVEN FOR THE FLOWERS
NEAR THE RIVER

1

The riverside flowers are driving me crazy
because there's no way to describe their effect

I went to see
my neighbor and fellow drinker

he's on a ten-day bender
all I found was an empty bed

2

Flowers in crowds, shoals, galaxies
swarm and tangle by the river

I don't walk I stagger
spring knocks me out

two things I can still manage
wine and poetry

you flowers
have pity on a white-haired man

3

A few houses here
where the river is deep and the bamboos quiet

but these flowers this red and white
flirtation

and what can I give in return?
spring, have some of this good wine!

4

Over to the east
Cheng-tu's flowers are lost in smoke

and Hundred Blossom Tower
has it worse

who can afford that place—wine in gold cups
dancing girls in plush surroundings?

5

Other side of the river
here's Abbot Huang's grave

spring light seems drowsy here
leaning against the breezes

a mass of peach blossoms
waiting to be picked

what do I want
a pink one or a red one?

6

Mrs. Huang's garden
flowers engulfing the path

thousands
weighing the branches

butterflies move pause move pause
it's a dance

and the orioles
know the appropriate music

7

It's not that I love them so much
I'm likely to die

but I know I'll age more quickly
when they're gone

clusters, don't wither and droop
so quickly

little buds, don't rush it
open slowly!

WEARY NIGHT

The bamboos creak with cold
I lie awake

the moon above the plains
fills one side of my garden

what makes this heavy dew?
countless tiny drops

scattered stars
come and go without warning

fireflies signal
back and forth in the dark

birds roosting near the creek
call softly to each other

ten thousand instances of war!
lost in it, awed by it

I sit up looking out
as the clear night wheels past.

SPRING

Rivers and mountains
in open sunlight

soft winds
among flowers and spice plants

swallows packing their nests with mud
ducks basking on warm sand

white birds mirrored
in the blue river

red flowers blazing
on the green slopes

I watch this rich procession
thinking, it's time I went home

WATCHING FIREFLIES

Fireflies from the Enchanted Mountains
come through the screen this autumn night
and settle on my shirt

my lute and my books grow cold

outside, above the eaves
they are hard to tell from the stars

they sail over the well
each reflecting a mate

in the garden they pass chrysanthemums
flares of color against the dark

white-haired and sad
I try to read their code
wanting a prediction:
will I be here next year
to watch them?

FIVE POEMS ON THE AUTUMN FIELDS

1

Day by day the autumn fields grow bleaker
and the cold river ripples the blue sky

I have moored my boat in a barbarous country
of mountains and constellations
and made my home
in a western village

when my dates are ripe
I let my neighbors pick them
when my sunflowers are choked with weeds
I hoe them out myself

an old man doesn't need much food
what's left on my plate
I scatter in the brook
to feed the fish.

2

When you come to understand the laws of nature
you see how hard it is to change them
deep water pleases fish
thick forest suits the birds

now that I'm old I accept
my poverty and illness
I know prestige and power
have burdens of their own

the autumn winds blow on me
indoors and out, table and walking stick
and I don't disdain
a meal of mountain ferns.

3

Music and ceremony to correct my faults
mountains and forests to addle me with joy

I nod till my silk cap
starts to slide off
the sun that warms my back
brightens my bamboo book

when the fall wind knocks down pinecones
I gather them
when the weather turns cold
I open the hives to collect the honey

a few last flowers here and there
I stop to inhale their fragrance.

4

In autumn the sand gleams white
on the far shore
the sunset reddens
the mountain ranges

hidden fish
break water
returning birds
battle the winds

the pounding of laundry echoes from each house
the sound of the woodcutter's axe is everywhere

I can do nothing to stop
the ministry of Lady Frost
her white blanket reminds me
how far I am
from the palaces of younger days.

5

I wanted my picture to hang
in the hall of fame, the Unicorn Gallery
now in old age
I waddle with the ducks and snowy herons

in autumn the big rivers rise suddenly
at night I hear
the waters roaring
in the deserted gorges

stones pile up to block the paths
the sail that might have carried me back
turns into a cloud

and my children grow up speaking
a barbarous tongue
as if they were only fit
for careers in the army.

WHITE HORSE

A white horse
comes running
from the northeast

two arrows
sticking up
from the empty saddle

and the rider
poor devil
who can tell his story now?

how his commander
was killed, how he fought
wounded, at midnight

so many deaths
have come
from this fighting!

I start to cry
my tears won't stop

LI HO

LI HO

Late in the T'ang period, there appeared a
poet so striking and so different that readers are
still not sure what to think of him. His name was
Li Ho, and his life (791-817) was remarkably
short. Unlike most poets of his time (though he
has this in common with Li Po), he did not be-
come a government official; although a brilliant
student and eager to prove himself, he was dis-
qualified from the official examinations through
a foolish technicality involving his name and
lineage. His subsequent life seems to have fol-
lowed this pattern: every day he would go out
riding on a donkey, accompanied by a servant
boy with a tapestry bag. As he wandered
through the countryside, he would compose
poems and toss them into the bag. At home in the
evening, he would dump out his day's work and
finish the poems, allegedly provoking his
mother's comment: "My son will not stop until
he has vomited up his heart!" This daily routine
was broken, we are told, only when Li Ho was
drunk or had to attend a funeral.

Li Ho's is a poetry of extremes. The images startle. The tone changes abruptly. Juxtaposition, a central principle of Chinese poetry, is explored to its limits. Mysterious timescapes alternate with the more familiar landscapes of Chinese literary tradition, though Li Ho's landscapes tend to be spookier than those of his predecessors. Something of the brilliant magic that charges Li Po's representation of the world is present, but in a much more melancholy and haunted form. At the same time, one would not want to suggest that sorrow is Li Ho's only note; the world and its mysteries clearly exhilarate him. This poet is very much an aesthete, drawn to curious artifacts, ancient legends, beautiful women (courtesans and dancing girls especially), picturesque ruins and strange rites. He is fond of letting the natural and the supernatural exist side by side, a rare taste in an age that liked to depict nature without any overtones of mystery or superstition, as in Wang Wei's landscape poems.

Li Ho also manages to be both present and absent in his poems, everywhere and nowhere, so that the poetry strangely combines the subjective and the objective; it is violently eccentric and at the same time transparent and timeless.

Li Ho is the narrator and protagonist of "Finding an Arrowhead on an Old Battlefield," for instance, but only so that he can serve as a medium (in all senses of that word) for the mysterious perceptions that transcend his personal experience and stretch the reader's imagination in several directions at once.

The use of extremes and contradictions, as well as the aestheticism and the biographical suggestion of the misguided genius who dies young, is more familiar to the poetic traditions of the West, and it may well be Western tastes and interests that have helped to promote a greater admiration for Li Ho's work in this century; for the Chinese he has always been too far from the norms of their tradition to be fully accepted as a great writer. Yet he has always exercised a kind of fascination. He has a legendary reputation as a gaunt and ghostly enigma, summoned on his deathbed by a heavenly messenger riding a red dragon. A common phrase for him is *Kuei-ts'ai*: demon-talented. And his literary influence can be found among many subsequent writers. One of them, Tu Mu, a ninth-century poet, was asked some fifteen years after Li Ho's death to write a preface to his collected poems. He tells us that he fudged and evaded the assignment, out of a sense of inadequacy. When he settled down to it, though, his enthusiasm took over, and his attempt to say why he thought Li Ho indescribable is both a brilliant description of the work and of the baffled and delighted response of readers over the years:

> Clouds and mist, mingling softly, cannot describe his manner; endless stretches of water cannot describe his feelings; the green of spring cannot describe his warmth; the clarity of autumn cannot describe his style; a mast in the wind, a horse in battle cannot describe his courage; earthenware coffins and engraved tripods cannot describe his antiquity; flowers in season and beautiful women cannot describe his intensity; fallen kingdoms and ruined palaces, withered grasses and grave-mounds, cannot describe his resentment and sorrow; whales yawning, turtles dancing, oxghosts and snake spirits cannot describe his unreality, wildness, extravagance, and illusion.

Most Chinese readers would feel that Li Ho does not deserve this book's implicit ranking with Wang Wei, Li Po, and Tu Fu. It is true that his career is shorter, his output smaller and perhaps more uneven, and that his intensity shows a more narrow range than his three great predecessors. But the quality of his imagination, which is one means by which we recognize the presence of poetic greatness, leaves no doubt in my mind about his claim to the company in which I have put him. He has a reach, a daring, and a command that take one's breath away.

Li Ho's work is represented in a number of anthologies, most notably A. C. Graham's *Poems of the Late T'ang* (Penguin, 1965). His complete poems have been translated by J. D. Frodsham in *The Poems of Li Ho* (Oxford, 1970). And he is the subject of a dissertation, a critical biography by Margaret Tudor Smith, *Li Ho*, published in Australia (Adelaide, Library Board of South Australia, 1967).

TWELVE POEMS ON THE MONTHS

First Moon (March)

I climb the tower steps
to welcome spring's return

dark yellow willow buds
the waterclock slow in the palace

mists curl in the fields
cold green
a bleak wind combs the stubble

asleep at dawn in her fancy bed
cool skin like jade
her dewy face still closed
turned toward the faint first light

you can't cut willow switches yet
along the roads, or tie
the leaves of the sweet flag together.

Second Moon (April)

Drinking wine by the ford
where they pick mulberries
dandelions blooming
orchids smiling
the leaves of the flag like crossed swords
swallows busy
screaming at the season
green dust
mist lingers in the rose border

her hair pinned up with gold
she puts the evening clouds to shame
her pearl skirts billow
as she dances

goodbye at the ferry
singing the flowing river song
spines chilled, tipsy
as South Mountain dies.

Third Moon (May)

East wind blowing
spring fills our eyes

city in bloom
the willows weep in earnest

breeze in the palace halls
and rustling the bamboo

new clothes, bright green
clear as water

a brilliant wind ripples fields
mile after mile

mist and cloud join heaven and earth

the concubines dress like soldiers
and paint their eyebrows thick

red banners warm the streets

the fragrance drifts away
down Meandering River
as pear blossoms
scattered in the park
make us think of fall.

Fourth Moon (June)

Cool dawns and dusks
lots of shade
a thousand emerald mountains
rising toward the clouds

a fragrant rain
patters through green foliage
thick leaves and blossoms
shine behind gates
water in the pools
quivers with green ripples

in heavy summer
blossoms expect to fall
fading red flowers
glowing in light and shade.

Fifth Moon (July)
Carved screens of jade on windows
gauze curtains across doorways

well-water drawn at daybreak
mallards and their hens
on painted fans

snowy clothes of the dancers
in the cool palace halls
sweet dews washing the air
sleeves flying
drops of sweat like beads of grain.

Sixth Moon (August)

Cutting raw silk
splitting flecked bamboo
we wear frosted robes
and lie on mats
as cool as jade

a flaming mirror
opens in the east
a glowing cartwheel
climbs across the sky
the Scarlet Emperor comes
riding his roaring dragon.

130

Seventh Moon (September)

Cold stars glitter
around the Milky Way
dewdrops gather on a plate
last flowers
open at the tips of twigs
orchids fade
in the empty, grieving gardens

the night sky is paved
with clouds like jade
lotus leaves in the water
are like green coins

on her bamboo mat
she feels the chill
through her thin skirt
as the wind beats up at dawn
and the Dipper curves down the sky.

Eighth Moon (October)

The young widow
lies awake and grieves
a lonely traveler
dreams he is home
the spider spins in the eaves
the lamp by the wall
makes little flowers of soot

outside, the bright moon
throws tree shadows through the screen

the dew goes everywhere
it even decorates
the lotus leaves in the pond.

132

Ninth Moon (November)

Except for a few lost fireflies
the summer palace is deserted

the sky is water

yellow bamboos
cold pools
dead lotus

the moon shines on the gold rings of the gates

chilly garden
empty galleries
blank white sky

frost walking in the wind
autumn leaves, gorgeous as brocades
in heaps along the roads

no watchman at the palace
to announce
the brilliant dawn

ravens croak by the brass well
as the kola leaves spin down.

Tenth Moon (December)

The arrow-mouthed jade vase
of the waterclock
will scarcely pour

the lamp forms soot flowers
but the light and its shadows
are motionless

icicles hang
beyond the gauze curtains

two rows of dragon candles
burn in her pavilion

under a pearl blanket
she lies awake

even in the robe
embroidered with gold phoenixes
she's cold

her eyebrows match
the crescent moon she stares at.

Eleventh Moon (January)

The palace walls
stretch away, quivering
in the cold light

the broken white sky
drops snow

ring the bells!
drink up!
this thousand-day wine
fights off the cold
drink your lord's health

the royal moat is frozen
the fountains are locked in icy rings

where is the fiery well?
where are the hot springs?

Twelfth Moon (February)

The sun's feet give off
a faint red glow
the rimefrost on the cassia branches
doesn't melt

now and then a warm breeze
tries to drive winter off
as the days grow longer
and the long nights end.

BIG SONG

1

The south wind
wears the mountains down
making plains

it's ordained
that the ocean god
will invade dry land
and leave the sea bed bare

when the Queen of Heaven's peachtrees
have flowered a thousand times
where will the men
of great longevity
and unrivalled wisdom
be?

2

A piebald horse
his neck dappled
under the dark mane

spring willows rising through mist

the lute girl
coaxing me with wine
in a golden cup

can blood and spirit
live together?
can they survive apart?

3

General Ting-a-ling
don't drink too much!
hero and master so seldom get together
I'm going to have silk embroidered
in memory of Ping-yuan
the lavish patron
and pour libations on his earth
for luck

4

That famous waterclock
the jade Toad fountain
drips too fast
chokes itself

the dancing girl's hair
gets so thin
she's afraid to comb it

the eyebrows of autumn
will turn green again

why do we waste ourselves at twenty
scrambling for positions
just so we can work for someone else?

AMONG RUINS

Daylight burns out
beyond the western peaks

blue moonlit clouds
bloom in the night sky

the past, the present
where is the end of it?

the wind has blown away
a thousand years

sands in the ocean
have turned to stone

fish blow bubbles
where the emperor built
his ruined bridge

to have come all this way
to find nothing but distance

and the bronze columns of the gods
long since vanished

SONG OF THE SCREEN

Butterflies lighting on carnations
silver hinges

a frozen pond
duck green
glass coins

six folded screens in a circle
around the orchid-oil lamp

at the mirror
she loosens her hair
dropping the gold cicada hairpins

warm fire of aloes wood
dogwood smoke

wine-cups from the wedding
tied together with a sash
her new pleasures as a bride

wind blows dew in the moonlight
cold beyond the screen

crows call from the city walls
the slim-waisted woman lies sleeping

MEDITATION

Sorrow on the mountain
a misty rain
falling in withered grass

midnight in the capital
how many men
are growing old in this wind?

evening   I get lost
on small trails that twist
through gnarled black oaks

straight overhead the moon
drives shadows back to their trees
whitens the hills with false dawn

torches
welcome the newly dead

over the fresh graves
fireflies!

DAWN IN STONE CITY

The moon's gone down
behind the high dike

a few crows fly up

dew-soaked crimson flowers
their cold perfume
cures my hangover

the Woman and the Herdboy
have forded the sky's river

willows filled with mist
hide the wall at the corner

the departing guest
leaves his tassel
a pledge to return

144

she frowns
her green smudged eyebrows meet

spring curtains of gauze
flimsy as a cicada's wing

a gold-braided bed
the shy flower of sex

willow fluff
shivers on the curtain
crane's down

no words can describe
the emotions of spring

MAGIC STRINGS I

The sun slips down
behind the western mountains
hills to the east vanish

the wind is driving horses through the clouds

the painted lute
and reed flute
play soft
rapid notes

a brocade skirt
rustles through
October dust

breeze flutters the cassia leaves
seeds fall

a blue fox
weeps blood
for her dead mate

riding the golden-tailed
dragons painted on ancient
walls, the rain god leaps
into the pools of autumn

a hundred year old owl
changes into
a forest demon

laughter!
green fire in the nest!

MAGIC STRINGS II

The witch pours
her libation, the wine
sizzles and clouds
gather in the sky

sweet fumes from the coals
in the jade brazier

sea gods and mountain demons
take their seats

votive papers crackle in the wind

her passion-wood lute
is inlaid with a golden phoenix
plucking it, she screws up her face
muttering
in time to the harsh chords

she calls the stars
and the dim gods
to her cup and dish
their feast

when demons are feeding
men shudder

the sun crawls over the mountains

the gods are all around, almost
visible!

their anger and pleasure leap
across her tranced, twitching
face

then they mount their chariots
and ride, a swirling host
back to their distant mountains

FINDING AN ARROWHEAD
ON AN OLD BATTLEFIELD

Black ashes, dust
powdery bones
red pigment stains

ancient blood
has flowered green
on the bronze

the white feather gone
the shaft rotted
only this wedge
this wolf's tooth

I was crossing the plain
with two horses
east of the outpost
through stony fields
and weedy ridges

early darkness
the strong wind died
a few stars
and wet black banners of cloud
hung overhead

ghosts cried out on all sides
I sacrificed some wine and mutton

the insects were still
the wild geese moaned, far off,
and the reeds shone red

a whirlwind
blowing foxfire
kept me company

I like to find old things
and I picked up that arrowhead
in tears, that broken point
that buried itself
once, in human flesh

but I traded it later
to a boy on horseback
in the southeast quarter
who begged to have it
and gave me
a new bamboo basket

A BEAUTIFUL GIRL
COMBS HER HAIR

Awake at dawn
she's dreaming
by cool silk curtains

fragrance of spilling hair
half sandalwood, half aloes

windlass creaking at the well
singing jade

the lotus blossom wakes, refreshed

her mirror
two phoenixes
a pool of autumn light

standing on the ivory bed
loosening her hair
watching the mirror

one long coil, aromatic silk
a cloud down to the floor

drop the jade comb—no sound

delicate fingers
pushing the coils into place
color of raven feathers

shining blue-black stuff
the jewelled comb will hardly hold it

spring wind makes me restless
her slovenly beauty upsets me

eighteen and her hair's so thick
she wears herself out fixing it!

she's finished now
the whole arrangement in place

in a cloud-patterned skirt
she walks with even steps
a wild goose on the sand

turns away without a word
where is she off to?

down the steps to break a spray of
    cherry blossoms

LI SHANG-YIN

LI SHANG-YIN

Li Shang-yin (813?–858) belongs to the late
phase of the T'ang. The dynasty was breaking
up. Royal princes were frequently murdered by
the eunuchs who controlled the throne and plot-
ted each succession. Provincial warlords were in
many cases practically independent rulers. The
whole era was marked by social turmoil, politi-
cal factions, and great uncertainty. Our poet
seems to have survived by attaching himself to
various patrons and by accepting whatever gov-
ernment posts, from librarian to sheriff to mag-
istrate, were tossed his way. His political and
economic fortunes fluctuated considerably, but
his literary reputation grew steadily. He became
in his lifetime and has remained one of China's
most admired and intriguing poets.

The first difficulty for Western translators
and readers in approaching Li Shang-yin's poems
lies in their unusually extensive use of allusion.
He draws from folklore and legend as freely as
from nature and his own experience. The result
is that the networks of imagery in his poems

usually depend for their fullest meaning on the reader's recognition of references to familiar stories from history and the popular imagination.

Compounding this difficulty is his tendency to work on several levels at once. Li Shang-yin likes to stretch his reader's capacity for simultaneity, risking ambiguity and frustration in the process. Poems that reach in several directions may seem to have no center. They can, on the other hand, be more satisfying in the long run than simpler lyrics. One result of the poet's interest in simultaneity is that the body of commentary on his poems is more fantastic, speculative and contradictory than is usually the case. The commentators often choose a single possibility — the poems are allegories of his relations with his patrons, or they are disguised accounts of his love-life, or they are veiled political satires — to the exclusion of most others.

A striking example of Li Shang-yin at his most difficult is the poem I have titled "A Riddle and a Gift." My colleague Dale Johnson once chose it for presentation to a translation class as an example of an untranslatable poem. His literal, character-by-character version reads like this:

Brocade curtain just unrolled, Lady of Wei.
Embroidered coverlet still heaped, Lord
    Ngo of Yueh.
"Hanging Hands" wildly dangle carved
    jade-girdle.
"Bending Waist" energetically flutter
    saffron-colored skirt.
Shih household wax candles when ever
    trimmed?
Hsun secretary's incense burner when
    needed perfume?
I am in dreams handed talent brush.
Want to write flowers leaves send morning
    clouds.

It is both a love poem and a complex set of
tropes that attempt to portray a peony. The first
line alludes to the story of a beautiful but
wicked concubine of Duke Ling of Wei. She re-
ceived Confucius while concealed behind a
screen; here it's as if she has suddenly decided to
make an appearance after all. The second line
refers to a story about a lord who was so moved
by the song of a boatman on a state barge that
he embraced him and wrapped him in his em-
broidered coverlet. The next two lines refer to

popular dances and also glance back to the opening lines, the first to the fact that the unseen Lady of Wei could be detected by the tinkling of the jade pendants on her girdle, and the second linking the saffron skirt with the quilt or cloak in the boatman story. The next pair of lines allude to the Shih household, so wealthy they did not need to trim their candles and even used them for kindling, and to Hsun Yu, a statesman who appears to have been so virtuous that when he visited a house the place where he sat remained fragrant for three days. Li Shang-yin next mentions the story of Chiang Yen, a 5th century poet to whom the poet Kuo P'u appeared in a dream, demanding the return of his magical writing-brush. He relinquished it and never wrote another decent line of verse. The closing line's allusion to morning clouds probably intends to evoke the story of King Huai, who lay with a goddess in a dream: she told him that the morning clouds and evening rain were manifestations of her person.

Out of this complicated web of allusions gradually emerges a fantastic portrait of a peony: its opened bloom, its leaves, its graceful movements in the wind, its blazing colors and rich scent. And the peony is, in turn, an elaborate compliment (and complement) to the lady, a gift to her and a mirror of her beauty. The poem, in effect, requests her favor. A. C. Graham's paraphrase of the close is: "I, who dream that I possess the gift of poetry which Chiang Yen dreamed of losing, send you this letter, figuring your beauty in the beauty of the peony, and asking you to favor me as the goddess favored King Huai." Thus lady, flower, and allusions to various anecdotes and wonders all resonate simultaneously in the compact system of the poem: the reader's anguish at puzzling it all out is meant to transform to delight when the entire design comes clear. It is indeed a riddle and a gift.

Not all of Li Shang-yin's poems rely on such dense and constant use of allusion, but the tendency to such reference, always present in classical Chinese poetry, is certainly more pronounced in his work than in most Chinese poets. What keeps a translator from giving up in despair is a sense of how much poetry actually does come through even when the poem loses some of the proper names and specific allusions that root it so firmly in its culture. I have often resorted to explanatory phrasing in place of proper names, inevitably sacrificing some of the poet's striking economy. And I have been encouraged by the way that the allusions, even when robbed of the resonance provided by their original time and place, retain a vibrancy and an ability to function as associative images in a highly imaginative poem. A translator requires considerable freedom to make all of this work. I have turned a bird that has been often translated as a cuckoo or nightingale into an American counterpart, the whippoorwill. I have risked the wrath of scholars by calling a highly ornamented lute "overdecorated." I have probably trusted too much to luck and my poetic instincts. My hope is that the versions I provide can stand on their own as poems, without footnotes or glossing. Readers who want information about the allusions that underpin them can readily seek out the more scholarly versions and discussions cited below.

If Li Shang-yin were merely a poet of complicated allusions and beautifully articulated structures, we would not value him as fully as we do. Along with the aestheticism and the delightful playfulness, we can find a depth of emotion and a sense of the fragility of human life and happiness that gives the poems a counterweight to their own exhilarating cleverness. This element becomes more pronounced as the poet moves into his central subject, human love: to a degree unprecedented in Chinese poetry, Li

Shang-yin is a student of the complex relations between men and women. The poems probably do not in every case record his own affairs and emotions, but the genuine passion and the unmistakable sympathy in them suggest that he is deeply preoccupied with human love and sexuality, a student of all the pleasures and pains that can arise in the course of infatuation, pursuit, loss and reconciliation. The group of five poems I have called "Untitled Love Poems" can thus be seen as central to his work and to this selection from it, but the reach of his interest in love is also reflected in poems like the three for the moon goddess and the ones on topics like fallen flowers and spring rain.

Because we know next to nothing about chronology in Li Shang-yin's work, my ordering of poems is conjectural. I have tried, though, to suggest what I think may reflect a course of development. "Things I Can't Stand Hearing" feels early to me, the work of a brilliant student. There's a similar, if slightly more advanced, quality to extravagant pieces like "The Over-decorated Lute" and "A Riddle and a Gift." The love poems, along with the adultery and moon goddess groups, feel like mature or "middle" work. There's a simplicity about "Fallen Flowers" and "Spring Rain" that may make them later. And certainly "In Exile" and "Letter Home" suggest late work, the achieved mastery of a poet who has learned exactly how economically he can capture powerful feelings. Taken all together, the poems in this selection seem to me to confirm that Li Shang-yin is no decadent versifier but a human and humane artist who feels deeply and sees deeply into the mysteries of our common existence.

Versions of Li Shang-yin's poems show up in most of the standard anthologies of Chinese poetry, such as *The White Pony* and *Sunflower Splendor*. A. C. Graham's *Poems of the Late T'ang* has a good selection and a helpful discussion. The book that looms largest, however, for anyone who wants to study this poet in detail, is James J. Y. Liu's *The Poetry of Li Shang-yin* (U. of Chicago, 1969). He translates and comments on 100 poems, surveys the various schools of interpretation, and provides many illuminating insights into the poet's life, canon and techniques. For my own versions, I am indebted to Dale Johnson for many helpful suggestions and corrections.

THINGS I CAN'T STAND HEARING

Gibbons screaming in the distance
as I sit in a deserted hall

the way people bicker and squabble
around the well at the market

the sound of laundry being pounded
at a wayside inn in autumn

a young wife
weeping for her husband

an old man crying
over his dead son

a magpie's screech when I've just come
from failing my exam

a neighborhood beggar
wailing all night long

somebody making joyful music
while I'm in mourning

news of a friend about to graduate
who died instead.

THE OVERDECORATED LUTE

This thing has fifty strings
and nobody knows why

each string and fret brings back
the lost and blooming past

the philosopher, dreaming at dawn,
and his counterpart, the butterfly

or the shamed, love-mad emperor
melting into the call of the whippoorwills

full moon above the ocean
pearls swelling in a sea of tears

the sun grows warm — in indigo pastures
fine jade begins to smoke

love should live on and on
filling our years and memories

but somehow it dazes us, fading,
and we're not even sure it was real.

A RIDDLE AND A GIFT

A brocade curtain parts: there's
the legendary beauty, Madam Wei!

embroidered quilts, meantime,
still cloak the boatman's shoulders . . .

or think of the slow dance, Hanging Hands,
and carved jade dangling from a sash

and the fast dance, Bending Waist,
with a fluttering saffron skirt!

colors flaring from candles
a rich man never thinks to trim

and fragrance like that of the holy man
who needed no incense or perfume . . .

I dreamed I was that poor poet
who got hold of a genius's brush:

wanting to create such leaves, such blooms,
that I could send to you

my lady of dawn clouds,
my peony.

UNTITLED LOVE POEM I

Your coming was a hollow promise
and your going left no trace

the slant moon clears the roof
the bell sounds out the hour before dawn

dreams of long separations
breathless cries, hard to get out

a letter written in haste
before the ink had time to thicken

candlelight on a golden quilt
with a kingfisher design

musky odors drifting through
lotus-embroidered bed curtains

Prince Charming already resented
the long trek to the magic peak —

now, range upon range before him
the mountains crowd the distance.

UNTITLED LOVE POEM II

The east wind sighs
and brings a misty rain

we meet by the lily pond
faint thunder in the distance

the gold toad bites the lock
that shuts away the incense

a jade tiger holds the pulley
of the rope above the well

remember the lady who peeped through the
    screen
to see the handsome young man?

remember the goddess who gave a pillow
to the famous prince of Wei?

hearts shouldn't try to be flowers
that just keep opening up

for every inch of longing
they make an inch of ashes.

UNTITLED LOVE POEM III

Hard for us to meet
harder still to part

it's true the east wind's stopped
but now the flowers have withered

the silkworm born in spring
will spin thread till it dies

the candle will stop weeping
only when it's burned down

mornings she looks in the mirror
to see if her hair has changed

evenings she chants sad poems
as the bright moon grows colder

the land of heart's desire
is never far away

bluebird, go find out the path —
show us how to get there!

UNTITLED LOVE POEM IV

The stars last night
the wind last night!

painted chamber to the west
cassia hall to the east

bodies are not phoenixes
to rise and soar away

hearts are linked by the magic line
that runs through a unicorn's horn

we played at Find the Button
sitting close in a spring wine glow

we acted charades on different teams
as the candles flickered red

oh no! the drum boomed out
calling me to duty

off I rode to the Foreign Office
a tumbleweed on the wind.

UNTITLED LOVE POEM V

Heavy curtains hang in the house
of the Woman of No Sorrows

lying in bed
feeling the long night's passing

a whole life in the arms of a goddess?
that was nothing but a dream

no lover has ever entered
the house of the Little Maid

indifferent waves and winds
punish the water chestnut

only dew and moonlight
can sweeten the cassia leaves

love is a total waste of time
you and I know that

but there's something about its madness
that opens the eyes and clears the mind!

DOUBLE POEM OF ADULTERY

1

In the darkened room just off the courtyard
a little drunk, they're lying down

think of the limbs of cypress and pomegranate
and how they grow and intertwine . . .

next to the yellow pillow
on the shiny bamboo mat

lies a loosened hairpin
and a pair of kingfisher feathers.

2

Dim white moonlight
light sweet dew

rooms like these
have seen so many meetings

when spring is in full bloom
birds are going to mate

husband, home from carousing
don't prowl around with a candle!

THREE FOR THE GODDESS
OF THE MOON

1

Deep in the mother-of-pearl screen
the candle lights its shadow

the Milky Way slips down the sky
and the morning star is setting

are you sorry you stole
the herb that made you immortal?

green sea, blue sky
night after ardent night?

2

The insects are deep in the grass
a light frost covers the leaves

this vermilion balcony
seems to oppress the shining lake

the hare and toad are chilled
the cassia flower is white

I think a night like this
must crack her heart.

3

Cries of geese going over
replace the sound of cicadas

the hundred foot tower looks out
over water that touches the sky

Moon Goddess and Frost Lady
can both withstand this cold

their contest is to see
who can produce more beauty.

SPRING RAIN

Moping in bed in a white coat
while spring goes on outside

the White Gate is desolate
and we seldom get what we want

I can barely make out the red chamber
through this cold rain

the beaded lamp sways slightly
as I come home alone

faraway roads are sad
in this spring twilight

waking near morning
confused by my own dreams

I'd like to send you this letter
and these jade earrings

one wild goose is flying
across a thousand miles of cloud.

FALLEN FLOWERS

The guests have all left
their high pavilion

and in the little garden
a whirling storm of petals

they lie in random heaps
across the twisting path

and stretch into the distance
to catch the setting sun

it breaks my heart
to sweep them up

instead I stand and stare
till they mostly blow away

these fragrant-hearted beings
going the way of the spring

they die and earn their tribute —
the tears that spot my clothes.

IN EXILE

A spring day
here at the world's end

the world's end where once again
the sun is going down

the oriole's cry —
if it had tears

it could water the blossoms
on top of the trees.

LETTER HOME

You ask when I'll be back —
I wish I knew!

night rain on Pa Mountain
overflows the autumn ponds

when will we trim the candle wick
under our own west window?

I'll be telling you this story
night rain will be falling.